THE MAGIC MAP OF ISRAEL

written by Ariel Batman

IN A TOWN WHERE THE SUN
SHONE GOLDEN AND BRIGHT,
LIVED NOA AND ELI,
TWO HEARTS FULL OF LIGHT.

THEY LOVED TO EXPLORE,
TO HELP AND TO LEARN,
AND HISTORY'S PAGES MADE
THEIR HEARTS BURN.

ONE DAY, WHILE PLAYING NEAR OLD CITY WALLS, THEY FOUND A MAP—COVERED IN SCRAWLS.

IT SHIMMERED AND GLOWED, THEN ROSE IN THE AIR, SWIRLING WITH MAGIC, BRIGHT AND RARE!

"TAKE THIS JOURNEY, FOLLOW THE PAST, SEE HOW KINDNESS CAN TRULY LAST." THE MAP THEN FLUTTERED, POINTED THE WAY, AND OFF THEY WENT —NO TIME TO DELAY!

FIRST, THEY LANDED WHERE
RIVERS RAN DRY, AND FARMERS
WOULD LOOK WITH A WISH
TO THE SKY.

THE FIELDS WERE DUSTY,
THE GROUND FULL OF CRACKS,
THE PLANTS WERE WEAK,
THEIR LEAVES TURNING BLACK.
BUT ELI THEN GASPED,
"LOOK OVER THERE!

A FARMER IS SMILING—
HE DOESN'T DESPAIR!"
NOA LEANED IN,
HER EYES OPEN WIDE,
"DRIP IRRIGATION!"
SHE CHEERED WITH PRIDE.
TINY DROPS,
SLOW AND SMALL,
SAVING WATER
TO HELP CROPS GROW TALL.

"THIS WAS INVENTED
RIGHT HERE IN OUR LAND!
A WAY TO GIVE NATURE
A HELPING HAND!"
WITH A WHOOSH AND A SWIRL,
THE MAP SPUN FAST,
AND OFF THEY FLEW TO THE
DEEP, DISTANT PAST!

HEALING THE WORLD,
ONE HEART AT A TIME
NEXT,
THEY ARRIVED IN
A HOSPITAL BRIGHT,
WHERE DOCTORS AND NURSES
WORKED DAY AND NIGHT.

PEOPLE FROM PLACES BOTH FAR AND NEAR, CAME TO ISRAEL TO HEAL WITHOUT FEAR.

A LITTLE GIRL SMILED,
THOUGH WEAK IN HER BED,
"I HAD NO HOPE,"
SHE SOFTLY SAID.
"BUT DOCTORS FROM ISRAEL
FLEW TO MY LAND,
AND GAVE ME CARE
WITH A GENTLE HAND."

NOA AND ELI BOTH
BEAMED WITH PRIDE,
"HELPING THE WORLD,
STANDING SIDE BY SIDE!
"THE MAP GLOWED AGAIN,
THE AIR FILLED WITH LIGHT,
AND SOON THEY
WERE SOARING,
OUT OF SIGHT!

NEXT, THEY ARRIVED
WHERE BRIGHT MINDS CREATE,
INVENTING NEW WAYS
TO MAKE LIFE GREAT.
A MAN WITH A CHIP,
NO BIGGER THAN A FLEA,
SMILED AND SAID,
"THIS CAME FROM ME!"

"IT HELPS BLIND PEOPLE,
IT HELPS THE DEAF,
IT GIVES THE WORLD HOPE
WHEN THINGS FEEL TOUGH."

A ROBOT THEN WHIRRED, "I HELP PEOPLE STAND, EVEN IF THEY CANNOT MOVE THEIR HAND."

ELI TURNED,
HIS HEART FILLED WITH CHEER,
"ISRAEL'S INVENTIONS
BRING HOPE FAR AND NEAR!"
WITH A FINAL SWIRL,
THE WIND SOFTLY ROARED,
AND BACK TO THEIR HOME,
THE TWO KIDS SOARED.

HOME AGAIN, HEARTS FULL

THEY LANDED AT DUSK,
THE MAP NOW STILL,
THEIR HEARTS WERE WARM,
THEIR SPIRITS THRILLED.
THEY'D SEEN THEIR LAND,
SO STRONG AND TRUE,
HELPING THE WORLD
IN ALL IT CAN DO.

NOA GRINNED,
"FROM WATER TO CARE,
TO SCIENCE AND KINDNESS,
WE LOVE TO SHARE!"
ELI LAUGHED,
"AND THOUGH WE ARE SMALL,
ISRAEL'S HEART
BEATS BIG FOR ALL!"

THE MAP GAVE A GLOW,
THEN FADED AWAY,
BUT THE LESSONS
THEY LEARNED
WOULD ALWAYS STAY.
FOR KINDNESS, ADVENTURE,
AND STORIES UNTOLD,
ARE THE GREATEST
TREASURES,
FAR GREATER THAN GOLD.

THE END

51600453R00017